Nova Lumina

poems by

John Doyle

Those eternal sources of light, love, passion, of the voice itself; may they shine, shine, shine...

On February 1st 2015, I doubted that at some stage of my life I would have written three books - certainly not ones that were poetic in nature. The following day I wrote my first poem in over 6 years while parked on a small country road near Kilcock in County Kildare. I can't even remember what the poem was - something about a mid-1970s styled Germanic looking house with a late arriving postman going up the driveway; whatever it was, I would like to thank that postman, and dedicate this collection to him; He was one of those lights I thought of when I wrote the lines above.

Le grá mór
Mother, Father, Annette.

Thank you to the following magnificent souls:

Marc Pietrzkowski, Andrew Clarke, Ken Folan, John Greene, Ivor McCormack, John Patrick Robbins, Michelle Goddard, John Harold Olson, Catherine Mulrennan, Pacelli Doyle, Nora and Onorio and Aria, Señor Carlos, Miranda Eilers, Paul Reilly, John Joe Doyle, Ned Connolly, Paul Brady, Luigi, Shivers, Richard, Mick "The Honourable Judge Herbert Nicholson is presiding" Deegan and everyone in VTOS, Dave "Davis O'Herlihy" Hurley, Amos Greig, Sean Ruane, Pat Doyle, Enda Carr, Anthony Smith, Alex Dempsey, Ruairí Ó Nualláin, Duane Vorhees, Ennis Magill, Gerard James Hough, John Warwick Arden, Chris McMahon, Paul O'Mahoney, John Reinhardt, Andy Lawless the music of Colemine Records, Mods, Rockers, (most of all Mockers), and God - regardless of what name you choose to call him, her, both, or all.
And all the poets online, offline, in flesh and in bone.

A few of these poems appeared in some shape or form in the following publications and websites - A New Ulster, Duane's Poetree, Your One Phone Call, The Rye Whiskey Review
Thank you to the editors of the above for their kindness and continued support.

Contents

No-one lights a lamp in order to hide it behind the door

—*Paulo Coelho*

The Wrens

A shovel's munch squelches - and winter's dip
frames our shrieking days - days where
irking Nordic fjords gash
through stiffened yard - stiff from ice
that marks the wren's affairs, daily -
the darts from flame-crisp brick
to furnaces of wild-fire fuchsia,
the handclap of drooping leaves
on crows' un-wanting claws.
In battalions they rustle dwindling plants,
October's auburn hood - more than vague and wordless cad -
and the wren's encore jives in lilliputian feet,
seeing,
hearing,
where Autumn, Winter, are pigments stung in squelching soil
leaving noon behind -
hearing
the choir of days descend;
We summon a gasp of spicy squash, a hastened blackcurrant and
blueberry slice -
days not as numbered as we once feared; the kitchen mumbles softly
in snow-smooth feet

We Never Go To Galway Anymore

Mortgages, kids, *"sorry, I'd love to, but..."*
mantras as common as a rolling knoll-grasped Westmeath road once was.
I had a fishing rod stored away
for years that reached past Shop Street, English girls with forgotten faces
to be cast in the glass-flat waters of *Recess* -
it lies buried - in bicycle wheels, electrical cords,
rusted in mortgages, kids, mantras of *"sorry, I'd love to, but..."*

The Fingallian Expression

I.M. Margaret Nolan 1896 - 1979

You were an oddball language,
so guttural in tone,
each jagged snipe
slithered under a wheat-hiss barn door,
each glaring dance-floor smirk
salacious in your Sunday missal.

My grandmother slipped under your spell
calling out those rockers in 1978,
go-boys revved up a frenzy on Laytown pier,
diesel-dirt leather rogues and her supine diphthongs
malavogued by *cinnits*
on the horse and carts to County Meath...

Réasúnaíocht

Sa fharraige
bí na focail ciúin i gconaí,

sa spéir
tá guthanna callánach i gcónaí,

i n-áit éigin i lár,
dún muid ár chluasa, agus oscail muid ár mbéal

Song for Annette

Night drifts us north;
we the toughened birds of Yukon, and Northwest Territories -
and starlight the softness that we need;

and I fall in love with tomcats,
like the hooded bandits orphaned - from the torch-lit shawls and saddles -
of Sandy Denny's April and August songs.

You're electric blue like the bronchioles of night,
and I like that: I like it a lot -
you and me, we've been born in sands that dare the wash of angry sea,

ghosts that dart and haunt the faces -
in lives from office blocks and drunken taxis -
that we may belong here

in the clasps of dipped Latin blue, the Da Vinci verandas
and the coolness overhead, that breaths and whispers -
wings over wood-shacked Yukon, eastwards until we stop at Yellowknife -

and Dublin - that's our corner,
the fold and rippled nest that Gods having
given us, hold and burn the bastard darkness
from this throbbing cobweb night

Coins

My caravans stretch forever in the hostel on *Francouzská,*
coins knitted on ringent window-cill
3 stories up - one slip - and the street owns my chapter's fiscal music;

we continue this trek,
San Francisco, *Chancellor Hotel,*
nickels stacked like hunchbacks in the wardrobe's tautened cubby;

When it's finders keepers and the coins' narrative stops,
Crusaders, Bedouins
somewhere, place worth on their sacred mount, the narrative's zinc

orated through
the sprints of sunlight, in Prague's *Francouzská,*
San Francisco, feeling tales of left-behind change chanting in Berber, long
sands of golden music

Ben Stone's Final Scene in *Law and Order*

So be it;
our sacrifice rubs its fingers up and
down Adam Schiff's shoulders,
a hunk of New York's finest porcelain -
like the priest leaves his Gods,
like the washer-women knead cloth through the clutch of adamant stone,
brittle, not short-changed on doubt.
Three blocks away
O'Flaherty's Bar and Pool Emporium
flashes Edison's electric blue, those midnight ladies whose
spinal cords arch in shapes of 80s hairspray rock,
5 years out of date;
He's Moriarty once more,
a wayward son's strung-up braces, an erstwhile villain
strung-up by half-faced smile, half-fade lights,
not porcelain made;
no, not even that strong

Sundown : Alicante Province

Two day stubble and sombrero soil
under orange-tree sunsets,
the hanging drift of day's cache of light
Orito, Montforte;

the adolescent olive trees
near the blurred red car
are stalked by sunlight
between

swollen glands of soil,
a few groves, whitewash ranches,
men in fields idle near JCBs -
and the highway's lemon-housed posse;

Novelda's church dares mountain to dislodge it from its perch,
the fields are elegies of browns,
of electric railway poles,
gorse fire smoke yet to be - perhaps enamoured

23/2/2018

Wheels

The monotonous sorrow of the finite...
—*Frank Bidart*

Their minds moved like wheels
but wheels became their minds,
something stopped moving,
something spun and spun,
but nothing there,
just bodies,
wheels,
an endless 2pm soap
where every cast-member thought they were smiling,
their smiles glistening on spokes
that once moved their minds,
that once meant something; yes, something

Nantosuelta

Tapping dandelion's
porcelain neck
she whisks these dipping evenings past -

as we did as weens,
scattering pods
as if some Roman sacrilege

in cracked tile
and marble,
broken face shattering the physiognomy of Pompeii,

a silence of watchers
as spiders cursed, then forgave
tufts of dandelion's hazy sway;

her June-time
Morse-code
dazzles buttermilk scorch

from
a low-hanging
porcelain Sunday,

she taps
a hurry of wilderness grass
as we do as marbled men -

Crew Hill,
mists of Moyglare,
sizzling, sparkling - this shoe-laced high-tension wire

The Lion in Springtime

Lesson One : Trust.
His hips extend - turbulent knees,
tilts as ships resuming steady water,
his eyes the starlight charts
skipper observes -
cargo safe, all crew sleeping, content.

Lesson Two : The Calm Azure Waters.
Like compass's unlatched lid checks skipper's aware
of knots we need, unwound in heavy-watered day,
a shore tingles with the spines of shipping forecast -
romance - Finisterre, Teutonic oars muscle German Bight,
finis terrae - a light warm to the prod of shaven shins -
and a lesson that prowls on and on

Corrugated Iron Fencing : Two Songs

first song :
A latch of plastic, much like what police
use for handcuffs these days
tickles and caresses its fencing
in remarks of stuttered breeze:
it makes percussive sounds:
it reminds me of that tingle that ignites Lalo Schifrin's *Bullitt* theme,
chiming its cobalt conspirators, off-kilter.

second song :
We watched the police attach those new-fangled
plastic handcuffs,
two men taken out, well, I say men, they were hardly 17,
broken-nosed, eyes gooseberry-puffed beneath
the shocks of expected teen-bravado;
the car looks remarkably well,
but the fence's song was stopped, nothing percussive, except
the deadened-music dragging wind
gave it.

Mother of Girl Missing After Terrorist Attack

I felt her heart - unbeating, like the
clueless half of God kerf its saints through the
lies of sonic mesh;
her hands weld in prayer
as if burned, *Petrus* shattered too;
I smell the acrid night's
ashen descents, the hours bring the same 4 note-jangle, a mea-
sured stone-swept voice.
Radio's switched off now -
I think of I, far too much -
silent as her, pebbles crunched in teenage pockets.
She's 15 years old, you keep on saying,
15 years old, in peach and sunrise shorts,
skin perhaps still as pink as evening - her most recent evening,
out among the rocks,
the lighthouse petrified, crumbled

Francisco Franco Strapped Up to a Space-Age Life Support Machine, November 1975

Whispers on the street - hell's guts shake, rattle, and roll,
fingers from faces gaunt, eyeless poking through, pinch mementos
from his skin;
he asks *how hard can it be to die,*
a sudden scorch of Gernika, the flesh of Barcelona, punctured
on the brittle calcium of his unilateral streets -
all quite ironic really, bones once used as drumsticks
for marching bands
shake, rattle, roll, in the music of his roaring silent death;

and Satan's cadence beeps in music-choking time

Did You See the Other Little Girl?

Mother asks; she
holds this squishy clump of daughter, sure it's the way Russia
would hold the Romanov quartet -

if given one last chance;
and she tells me, by stealth
the girl's much-whispered

name,
it stuns me like bullets
that stop breath reaching me,

but mine perhaps deserved.
I spoke her name in French, yes perhaps she's beautiful;
I've thought too much of mothers, of daughters recently.

The laws of attraction in turn tried to butcher me today,
bury me alive in a post-war forest where trees do everything to hide stars
and the graves lie shallow -

men in cloth caps smoke while digging, like its a means to an end -
nothing that has any profound meaning,
like little girls named in French after mothers who maybe sometimes
are beautiful

and hunt me by stealth -
and tap shovels on mounds of earth,
with an assured satisfaction,

Citroën vans smoking the fear
from sunset,
chugging the wasted guilt away

County Fermanagh

The curlew siphons Tuesdays
from lake's decanter song,

morning scoops
remnants of dawn

from the lake's
stiffened shrine of weed;

a few cars pass,
the engines' hum picks ears from sheaths of screeching grass,
all as masts un-bending

County Carlow

Bagenalstown;
inches from our clasp;
these ballad-singer signs
mutter *Muine Beag - i nGaeilge*,
in brands that read like ancient scrolls -
one of landed gentry, the thunderclap of horse and cart,
the other - of native serfs, clothing ripped on
sanguine briers;
making contact - fingers taunt escaping sun
and names of pubs like 1940s westerns -
John Ford's recline in t-bone shoulders
propping-up a glow-filled bar; glowing, emptied.

Rains are trotting fast this evening, we note, then park near
the old town hall,
grazing leaves
as consuls of light
in towns where petrol pumps
form armed guard,
and the nickel-coloured rains
fall like bullets
from Ford's *Americana* pocket;
prospectors lined-up,
pans emptied of promise;
in County Carlow
the hills are suffused in citrus evening's death;

we'll ride on, do we agree? - begging gold
from slot machines
in snake-oil chip-shop windows?

Bernhardstraße, Dresden, June 9th, 2010

Poked through whirlwind leaved-horizons
eager windows
and a girl's keyboard notes recharge;

a city's perspective
sparkles electric-kinetics
on these terracotta-skinned tiles

and those Morse-coded stations an hour swished past -
Bad Schandau, Děčín - they seem like that piano
pattering note for note on the opaline smile of rails - but now the street

and the European summary of green
have me as willing and bowed acolyte,
a girl's staccato notes swaggered in ivy - on these concrete battalions.

I know how beautiful you are, *fräulein,*
your arms tempered like China-cups in furnace,
knees touching chest, tightened gait of bus - in tune with glass-milk sun

Liechtenstein

Beauty is God's handwriting
—Ralph Waldo Emerson

I would kiss you for your name, for breath alone,
Germanic lilt of ice-caked stone,
that rocks me to my bones,

the searing blue
that breathes a chill
through rivers

like dreams I've had
in postage stamps, tea-towels, and
photographs thinner than star-kissed air -

the curve of valley
like pregnant hips - its stomachs
ovulate in the sighs of cloud

Coda

He moves his fingertips
up and down his concubine's spinal cord
as the guy on stage pours his heart out like Dennis Wilson.

She does not return his serve. She's looking at the ball-boys; oblivious

Ralph

For Ralph Sanyaolu

Probably I'll meet you - in a dockside bar in colonial Kuala Lumpur
with chiming bikes on the slips of cobblestones
and the economic movements of fish outside in urgencies of size nine feet;
your face gives the bar something to think about, as it tries to knock
its many lives into shape,
and then you'll say "as I live and I breathe" when you greet me, the whiff of
pineapple
from your tropical shirt cutting through the aggression of oriental Captain
Quints, and the seven day throb of size nine feet;
maybe

Gamekeepers...

...or culprits, no surprise really, that they
stalk greenhouses in episodes of *Randall and Hopkirk Deceased*, that they
hold the former Mr. Lewis Brian Hopkin Jones face down
in sublime waters,
mustache, shotgun held half-opened;
and gunpowder spooks me
like the hopeless signals that brewed an afternoon in Campania -
furnace spits bullet in one trajectory,
the other half two choices, where dead men bubble in mirrors face down,
where P.I.s flirt their loves and last life of nine, down the barrels
of a gamekeeper's jealous gun - culprits amassed. The young heiresses'
hands coyly clench in guilty pockets; Jeff Randall's bones black and blue
like dusk, on the cold silence of floor

They're Not Bad Bastards, Those Rooks

Pecking - the altar boy make his breakthrough -
a clutch of divinity successfully transported,
followed by teenage scratching,
a wobble, Gene Vincent hair, black as the edge of time.
They sail morning's breath of yawns,
sail on high-sheaths of land - I watch them
gather twigs in tandem
that shakes a torn-paged rustle, shades of brown
I watched splash before me, in the love-rationed depths of County Meath -
when in October - and Tony and Kate's dog Bobby still had best of health.
Rooks are charred fawns, feathered in their deaths,
their rejects tipped, splattered -
on diamond-cuts of gravel.
I hear three rooks baritone from their Grecian-circled mound,
near the applauding lap of cold-stiff river -
it seems their dead sometimes fly, sometimes
flight tricks our mist-pecked eyes, Bobby's vigil heats their trail,
alas Gene Vincent though - a solo-flight among many

Watching the Cricket, Trinity College Dublin, 2/6/18

Ah, those evenings -
where Mick Jagger's cotton-cooled angel
surfs the powdered-blues of Lords,
London's smog and soot clueless outside;
I read those papers, and dreamed of you and me
sipping pims, and the skeletal girls in hopscotch slacks
who rub their strings as songs begin, sit on dusty beer-filled steps -
and end
on the slap of ball on bat, and boys walk past, l.b.w. - yet again;
but that's ok, a witness of you and me, of Jagger, the thinnest cut of
woman
clenched to her guitar, and the angels are cool and chilled somewhere;
in newspapers in 1976 -
when Summer knew exactly what it was supposed to be

The Horse-Boxes With Their Northern Ireland Registrations Drive Past

April - our first matinee,
akin to Nureyev in full-flight -
a sky's powdered desire
swept lust through council homes,
the lanky-trousered suburban bus gawking;
I stand by these allotments
(like Spain, they keep their calmness, nothing ventured,
breeze and home-brew gained),
that highways and bothered trains merely glance upon
as if April was sired by them alone.
 By Mr. Galvin's farm
 the lasting Carton clench
 weakens, giving leeway
 to sunshowers, to passing horsebox, *Down, Antrim* registration;
and the foreign taste of yellow those uppercase consonants
dazzled us with
in a time of little leeway,
spooked and shuddered colts,
April's ice-breath calm much quieter, than the push and squeeze
of dormouse,
than Autumn's men who smiled, cycled past, trouser-legged
lamp-shade clinging.
I see our lives pushing pins and curtained skin,
skies fold like rising cake
in shapes of
coughing day, the sunshine yellow, the registration *foreign*, jaundiced -
and the horses are lined in shapes of two, perhaps for cyclists
to squeeze between, for the buses that poke their nose from Dublin -
leering; the chatter a sudden *Augustine*.

The Train From Leuven to Brussels

Offerings exchanged -
mine, a detailed sketch in Irish
that crackles this lyrical lipless kiss,

and yours -
that entrancement in Walloons,
aniseed strands, apple-hair,

Ardennes bicycles parting hill-side fords
in June - six months from now.
We use fog on carriage windows as parchment,

the language smells of Christmas markets -
Brussels creeping like clouds
that open rough-cut rope-sacks in November,

that grab summer's children
when trains slow-down.
If you speak your trance somehow, I'll hear your choirs,

even clenched in the fumbled bones of brittle city

December 2013

Case Studies for Matter of the Heart

There's a girl on the train reading Norman Mailer,
I'd say she's half-past 19 years old, *good for you*, I think;
a man 3 seats down lays half-asleep,
and judging by his poise I'd hazard
he's thinking about the blonde from *ABBA* -
around 1979 just when she got it right, not awful double denim,
just when they almost stopped being dorks;
and the girl who's probably 19 does look a lot like *Agnetha Åse Fältskog;*
if I could make their fingertips touch I figure I could start something
that looks like the Northern Lights over those places you see
on Canadian nature documentaries in technicolour from 1952,
with lightning and colours that know of each others' presence - revel
in the good natured competition -
something Mailer may not admit he would approve of,
but I'm sure he could find words for what I believe I can do
as I know she's not quite right for me,
but hell, I like this guy, there's something that he's got, I just can't explain

The Dandelion Woman

We chop and wreap,
trotting through the scrunch of
aeons - and thus
her panorama never tilts too far from Earth,
our peach and raspberry Earth,
or a sudden poise
to a lilted sun -
her Slaneyside songs and *Yola* brogue,
her pods' explosions on crosswinds, and the parish priest
with the surfeit of syllables, and the
dandelions beneath our advance -
chopping, reaping.
You were that song, that ventured forth our
Newbridge Sundays,
an encore's scrunch of aeons
and another primal scowl,
your song and alphabets,
amplified through aeons still.
And the things that make us happy are numbered thus -
a head count of sand on Curracloe Beach, 1986,
that perfect pitch of alto -
Ave Maria - Joan Sutherland? perhaps it was Callas?
you blessing the sleet from me -
pummeling Athgarvan village, January 1982,
like the bosch descent on Wexford, 1941,
my amber cheeks still sting of freelance shrapnel,
but vibrant next to your face.
And we count the dandelions
across Brownstown fields,
numbers exchanged
for one more cry, then a lamb-like coo,

to the sudden whisk of
Yola pun,
dandelion seeds
paused in slow motion -
as your casket fuses peach and strawberry earth

April 2016

Dexys Midnight Runners, 1980

Soul-tang
taste of tarmac

bites -
and the lungs of London, Dublin, Detroit

inhale;
and you breath in tone, in tempo,

tasting tarmac,
pickets, oil-drums with fires roaring up from Hades,

hands warm,
hands clapping, council workers' jackets

Man In The City
For a man they never found

He smiles in supermarket aisles,
his face drags along in post mortems soon after -
on faded cctv;

he walks a street that slips and slides from Sundays,
the listless leaves clamped on sports car windows,
soul music lost and found - on nearby antennas;

they'll find his face someday,
pressed on beds of murder, an emptied 50 cent novel,
a half-full gin bottle -

and the lights switched off in shopping centres,
feet muffled
in a dying swoosh of listless-leaves.

They watch his face press a cctv screen -
screaming, laughing;
the city's finest whipping boy - blackness burning detectives' marriages
- to a point of no return

I Think of Roland Barthes

For Sean Ruane

As traffic haunts the ups and downs of the stomach of the well-fed city,
curled like sleeping pythons around signs, signals, pizza-bar neon lights,
there is this old man - ripe for an engine's growling inquisitions -
I think of Roland Barthes, and I put language in its cage, where it will
fend for itself, live off wildflowers, weeds that poke through,
learn to be itself.
I will lay a wreath in Cherbourg, a name flavoured
by the sweet flowers of northern France,
climate mild, the chariot-crash of Rome's indulgence,
unrecorded, a cage unlocked.
Perhaps the cage has an engine, the chariot has four wheels,
and the ribs from the body
that housed the words of the absent mind - were too deep in thought,
too in love
with the language of its neon signs -
to translate the silence of the muted-brutal wheels;
Perhaps?

Stereotypical Strange Child Stares at Me in Local Cafe

His face stretches dangled greyness,
a displeased Wednesday seems
annoyed by showers.

Is *he* annoyed?
this phallus of bruised and snot-splashed discourse -
that I block his vista

to lands and riches
igniting a car park's
stone-clenched sombrero;

Somewhere
his parents park and then forget;
he - grey and stretched like an evening without its yellow bouncing
ball, yellow-martyred scowl

The Canal : Winter

(1)
The canal froze somewhat last Tuesday,
  firm enough for robins to press their police-precinct profiles,
    perch to dishonour their fastidious death.

The stricken branches abseil then stall;
     magpies pecking their nickel-toned flesh
       to a currency of their own calculation.

(2)
The thaw ghosted downstream last Thursday -
  Robins' innocence left unproven,
    and the magpies know dustbins cannot replace

  nests already full by the icy grip on eggs,
    webbed fossils that forensics see
      washed and numbered as zero.

(3)
Rafael holds his mother's hand
     then dips a little towards the water,
       the perch's carcass causing a curiously endearing squirm

The Canal : 2nd of June

When they say *deep water,*
trivialities such as death fade, to a few popped-up bubbles,
a dabbling duck, unconcerned -
I'm the *flaneur* flickering
in amphibious green,
though I will succumb, (just like everyone) -
to summer's lilting wings.

The waters are so murky
subterranean adjectives come alive,
like a monster from 1957 B-Movie depths -
The Beast From the Green Lagoon -
starring Clint Walker and Barbara Bel Geddes...

If death has certain beauty, shimmering silent
in forlorn peace,
the let me
play my leading role
about 55 years from now -

Clint Walker and Barbara Bel Geddes
sit under small cocktail umbrellas
in their passing punt,
me, fiddling cane, as if I were
French, deep in sluice-gates of thought,
and somewhat immortal;
Somewhat...

Robert Mitchum Spent a Little Too Long on the Ground After Falling Off His Horse

Light falls -
at first in ribbons, like
those split between leaf and withered branch, like
Eve's cuttings, as Adam
gathers round flags near shorelines, on
gurgling dreams, on times of clinking glass to come -
and then a sudden roar of exile -
where moon licked its broken beads
on sea,
and yachts glowed in bubbled shards
of light, their
days and sins could no longer afford.

The movie I watched last night was called *The Wonderful Country,*
in it I felt Robert Mitchum stayed down far too long, even though
his leg was broke, his steed
detached from the furlongs of life;
and I thought of Mitchum softened by sea, in Dún Laoghaire,
with Adam and Eve,
and the Lutheran theology of Ben Sterner,
to get them back on the straight and the narrow,
like a splint down Robert Mitchum's leg,
like that path near Dún Laoghaire harbour, once a railway siding,
I think -
horse clopping its water-baby sins behind. Stay down Bob,
grimace, no more trains will come, not since 1980

The Ice-Cream Man

His homicides are sudden music,
a promise that plunges steel
through the lungs of dying day -

and with Wagner being worm-food
it's La Cucaracha
that stirs his Valkyries to war...

Song for Harold Lloyd

Harold Lloyd,
you're a pinball
stuck in grid-iron fields,

kicking field-goals
for the girl of your dreams,
glasses half-steamed,

as the game comes to its Charleston slacks and shoes finale -
the universe lies exposed
in twinkling stars on Mildred Davis's sunrise cheeks.

Harold Lloyd, 1928,
girls in flappers run to you,
the rising of cool-cool steam, a nickelodeon of future dreams

Cabaret and Bingo

When places are actively sensed, the physical landscape becomes wedded to
the landscape of the mind
—*Keith Basso*

It lay flat among the unknown - who (or what) Cabaret and Bingo were,
Cabaret was a fabled Texan gun who ushered death
through bullets soaked in tequila,
Bingo was a place where adult men in dicky-bows grinned like rats
in mustached hedges, their women-folk stabbing disco
floors in strappy shoes.

Words and self take note -
Apache gospel glows.
I watch planes taking flight for France,
a secretary called Lorraine is dozing off on-board,
sozzled in Burgundy wine -
her disco shoes dangling loose, a moment - a person fixed in place,
a figment spelled by time

People I've Observed Recently

(1)

A chew n' spit pair of Cuban heels stare me down; scuffed, muddied -
John Wayne takes on Ronnie Corbett -
Alicante station, tourist info desk;
otherwise the shoes look good, Mod's approval,
mid 1960s cut.
English is their *Lingua Franca*,
Sergio's knuckles knead decades from his teak-stressed desk,
and Carl, (though perhaps Karl, explaining he's Czech
most certainly not German).
I wait - 25 more seconds, I'm gone, a bus appears, it
looks unwilling to gather the city's rising dust.

(2)

Management and Cost Accounting
by Colin Drury is like a baby kangaroo
squeezed between her breast and oxter;
A studious type, weekend scars do not appear -
like a mistimed yawn, a carnal celebration
smiling through the pressing rays of light,
the grace of windows, untested.
Some friends appear, they approach their seats directly,
four teas and a cool-gripped clutch of Coke scrutinise her digits,
numbers accounted for, the mind primed for sums of Sunday's temperance

(3)

Sergio León rejoined Real Betis last summer;
I've never been to Seville.

I remember Sergio León
one Spring Sunday, like a magnet, the grass dipped around him,
five guys swarmed like dive-bombers, I turned and faced the bar,
sipping brandy, I returned, he was gone, shadows
and the silent fate of steadied groans mourned his disappearance,
me, stiff upper-lipped, chilled,
him, a shuffled morning closely held to an airport runway;
Sundays are the days we should meet -
the economists and the tourists, the footballers and the Flâneur,
in cantinas in Seville

John Huston's Adaption Of *The Dead*

Thinness, it's colours argent cold -
Dublin, 1980s - the closeness of our hand-carved homes,
closeness as in *Radio 1* in the catacombs of night before Ireland shuts its
dreaming down -
and everything Huston touches has the tight-clenched feel of night
with closedown on radios and tv sets, so Dublin has its silence
to itself, and McCann's tenor's
tightness on the starched luminous white
reminds me when I saw *The Dead* 25 years later,
somewhere in South County Dublin, and everything was dead,
the more we moved,
and pressed buttons, and made it snow, in
Marie Keane's four-poster death,
in tall ornate rooms with fireplaces and mantelpieces
and the contentment of petrified nudes across Dublin, Wicklow,
in archways in Kildare,
in snowblind headstones, and the thinness Huston saw in stars
that mistook starched shirts for snow,
McDermottroe, Craigie, Donnelly, Carroll -
if we added Scott Fredericks it would be our Shipping Forecast -
a broadcast on the soggy death of lands, a requiem-mass closed down

Aftermath of a Ransacked Hotel Bedroom
(Galway, June 1997)

Ocean - once obedient - firstly you observed me,
yet now you police my thoughts,
Poseidon - I think your presence is more than close enough;
I'll slip my removals of self behind these battered *currachs*,
liminal guard to Grace and Katie's
lives -
etched in sand in childhood hearts - a
refusal to
budge, from this loudmouth (and illiterate) dank of sand.
And these sole-poke stones
stand jagged, damp - timeless like the broken arms on necklaced clock :
sisters' words and meatless weed -
a fantasy world
brewing clock-less storm - inside my elbow-squeezed untimed skull,
ocean returning its fingers to New York, though still peeking; my eve-
ning must resume somehow

What a Strange Strange Man

His wife's bones he loved to death,
all the world twisted from his shadows into his morbid grotesque stage,
an actor, eternity's sand-faced clown -
watching the shovels dig his only curtain call

Joke

It was a hard hard shoulder, they said,
a season's sliding road, and the cracks of winter fire
that tingled lines in splints of bone,

coming down hard
with mountain air
softened in yearning lung,

but your mind not at ease,
your body at several odds,
and your soul bulged between two poles;

like you and me
the sweat of handshake
means nothing

like the crack of bone
or tar-stick road,
coming down like Achilles

wheels still spinning,
and your softened handshake
loosens grip;

there are harder roads to crack on softened bone,
like me
who sees you, see me, thinking

that maybe I'm not thinking,
but I see you, and there's nothing there
beneath, between, beyond -

the crack of roadworthy bone.
These are the medals you'll see -
some among us cannot wear - or could not care

The First Time I Missed a Bus (Late 1982)

For Bob and Anne Levins - R.I.P. February 1987 and May 2013

So this is darkness
- *in the flesh* -
as common tongues assert,
you were that stranger teachers warned me of,
now I'm stiffened nude
in nocturne's growl,
bled by shards of dying sun.
This is what night-time looks like,
its noise and tribes oh so different,
punching my whole life banana-black.

This is me, a passing laugh on butcher's hook,
Lacan's artifact again -
on sullen shop-front glass.
This repose of evening chills strangers
on white-cold slabs,
and a meander of winter-shocked boys looking towards me -
to them I'm some sort of shaman, a guru to guide them back to
camp -
pining for a battered and elderly bus;
and how can I even tell them - I lost the firewood and quenched
the choking flickered lamp?

On Viewing *The Death of Cleopatra*
(Painting by Jean André Rixens)

Drapes - masonic in tone,
seem to breathe, and their secrets are not worded
in the mathematics one would expect;
there are rituals too, in the actions of the living,
invincible, foolish, learned too late,
ritual in the murals of death, that mourner and soldier
paint - common in tone, whitewashed like un-suffered body,
leaving space now, for the common codes of creeping black

Returning from Kilcloon, April Evening

We inhale these town's smiling rivers -
all of them - *Lyreen, Joan Slade*, a simmering *Rye*;
and the curlew's chuckled prayer
rotates the neck-tie washing lines,
telegraph poles garters like the sheet music sunset promised.
I'm sure you've got a thousand poems for me, baked-scone
evening -
I'll take just this one
and let it breathe all around me - farmers all content;
the rattling tractors making precise - the arrangements for
their concertos

Nell Mangel from *Neighbours*

Make no mistake -
communities need *more* like her,
her petite maneuvered s-hook shape
watering flowers at the fronts of
Melbourne gold-rush houses. Damn it, we'll dig up her if she's dead,
get her d.n.a. and plant millions like her among those flowers,
the bumble bees buzzing on chit-chat of mullet-haired boys,
and a sharp-shard of silence that executes the moment -
when rock n'roll
hot-rods rev-up - two doors down;
No-one really saw Nell in 1975,
when all her husband wanted to do
was read his paper, watch the horses on tv; and she watched Bon Scott
and Malcolm Young stroll past,
laughing, kissing girls, and turning around to gloat - those *bad bad boys.*
Her purple-frocks and tumbleweed hair
led the cavalry from Sunday schools
straight to an ice-cream parlor -
Nell Mangel
singing *Onward Christian Soldiers* -
and we miss the liquorice, milk and peppered old-bag,
and *Hiace* vans driven by well-mannered boys called *Brett*
who would deliver carpets and sit-down for tea,
and she would unexpectedly cry...

Squalls

Squalls squabble -
Sardinian words sanded on the tangs of newly-tasted tongues -
Scirri, mannu - oceans roar these terms with fearsome affection -
The Greater Scaup, The Eurasian Wigeon - its floating dialects -
Squalls rising - unended

Walking the Dog
I.m. Burt 10/1/2002 - 30/3/2018

He's older now,
call it as it is -
Elderly's a word that
means smiling, boiled stuck-together
sweets-giving women,
skulking skinny few syllable sharing miserable men.

He's older now,
not tugging the divine strength of Job these days,
it is you
who serenely
dislocates his shadow;

and when he wants to Sherlock
some shit and piss
leave him be -
this being his *San Tropez*, his seaside day-trip
on a bus of sweets-giving ladies -
men silent to their skin-hung bones, who
suddenly fall in love...

No-One Returns Borrowed Books, Ever

Though perhaps death may share the blame -
I fail to accept logic, reason, sorrow as excuses;
my Herman Melville, my *Readers Digest Guide to Better Gardens, 1972,*
are these merely bystanders to a shard of sudden stroke that bites the
lives from a clutch of barbed-wire chests,
that flinch at the snap of slipping bone
on the shiny tiles of clickety-clack suburban homes - white wine everywhere?
No, I believe not.
I peer through the tortures of whipped-tight blinds,
of lights ashamed to be clothed in the scarlet sins of red,
I see my pile, and they see me, the bridge of death and darkness
ropeless in-between;
Jump I say, *jump* I tell them, perhaps they'll die too,
my curtain's love for glimpsed and clutched
street-lamp light
as wordless and un-edited as ever

Greenfield Chimneys

For Anthony Smith

The speech of smoke tickles drizzle
sailing down whiskey-brown

Edinburgh

9/12/2011, 3.44am

John Shea,
BBC Radio 3,
a bedroom that conducts its strings

in neon gallops of nocturne snow; *Kingsway Guesthouse -*
Nick Drake's At *The Chime of a City Clock*
in the heart of a girl giggling below; and the colours -
liquorice blue, intermittent

Eze Graveyard Cote D'Azur, France : Three Songs

L'Enfant Daniel Brogna 1952 - 1953

I can tell their visits have decreased, each stone around your grave
kissed by weed, each drop of rain adds a swollen Franc to your
threadbare pockets.
Stillness and silence, it's rate of exchange barked and clumped in the
futures of stooping wall.

Ici Repose Mon Regrette Cher Tamagno Berto

The worker bends his bones, an inscribed plaque upon you
shows me how - he cuts and digs, cutting, digging deeper,
for I feel he wants this earth to hold you, as though your shapes
may be stone now,
it is soil that holds and radiates your warmth. And a rose
blooms without border,
he and she - its petals.

The Bridge of the Devil

I think of Tony Curtis and Roger Moore, dicking around
the south of France,
1971; I've found a corner where solace hides - depending
on the shape of sun
and how the clouds choose to interpret - though algebra, perhaps a more
guttural Gaulish science - soothing stone, coin-toned silver,
that crisp cough of trowel
poked between rock and mortar, and Curtis and Moore,
hundreds of feet above,
riding with the devil in the heavens in 1971

Sherlockstown, County Kildare

The drunken trees
tightrope the swarm of stout and well-fed cloud,
poles in fields around us, creosote dribbled; the electricity of bees
gathering, the snip of surgeon prunes the soft thickness of adolescence,
the clutching music snaps - conductor cleans baton, shirt sleeves
shortened

Some Things Ray Davies May Consider Adding to the Village Green Preservation Society Master-List

Football commentators who sound like they're talking down a telephone line in a stadium with a running track, gas horns and Sport Billy and Iveco advertising hoardings

The Phillips Test Card

Bratislava side street cobblestone cafes in vanilla streetlamps

Walking home slightly-drunk on English ale in the fresh chill of snow, orange light, the clean flump and crumple of feet underneath

The sound of morse code and the commentator going bat shit crazy as Tardelli scores...

All Those Cars

The little scratch of twig
on coughing folds of fog,
the hallowed hounds of headlights
hunting

Combine Harvesters near the Lumville Hotel, County Kildare, August 1978

Beauty is not caused. It is.
—Emily Dickinson

Horse brass chings -
it's Sunday;
barley's wheat-cured folds of firm golden giddy-haired girls
awake
in the maelstroms, in the meadows, between; and this
entourage of combine harvesters prowl the manly muscle
of eloped terrain
near the necks of shapes the elderly barley's
signatures calm and caress, making us, remembering -
we, the gold of sun, and Gods yet to be worshiped, sacrificed

On Reading *Westmeath* by Frank McGuinness

(Local Park at Leinster Cottages Maynooth County Kildare, March 2018)

Frog fossils sire worshipped stone,
the lime green blotches
moving three by tree;
much like death, it keens those fabled triplets -
of drug and bacchus honeyed superstars;
So it's March, you say, and
the landscape
unconfirmed, slobbers its rural slurs in survey vans,
the frog-spawn greens on heads
of nipple-tipped shivered stone.
These vans no doubt grumble
on roaring intersections,
maps stinking with uncouth Celts
levering across the pools of snowy water -
stone that comes to life you tell me, awaits the vans
with men in slacks and beards who will soon arrive, to flick their
cigarettes and clutch these
paper/scissors/stone lives - memory, stone, the leaping loving
greens, soaked in verdant land
frozen, sometimes thawed on baggy grabs of map

On Viewing *Crimson Dusk* - Painting By Mo Kelly

The poppy fields of France, of Belgium -
have we seen them clutched in snow, out of breath
for the winter's swirls and swoops? sometimes yes,
in lives like these, where the sun weaves and whirls
like enraged genie, like bottle smashed on boy's shivered and slivered
floors;
The poppy fields, (though Celts may become inflamed), drowse like
furnace,
hum like dawn's patent ruby feet,
whites, greys, browns, the crests of frosts, rains, the love and light that
rumbles like worm making love in clenched-thickened soil;
and the music, that too - weaves and spins, tuning reds in keys of
ankle's squelching earth,
feet on floors in domes stiffened - in the clutch and cloaks of fire-
breather's reds

Bill Evans Moves at One with His Cosmos

Bill Evans; chin meets head, meeting a whole world
bowed - his tabernacle
typing codes -

descending,
          ascending;

breathless huffing puffing bass
runs like fat man that final second late - for the vicious yelping
train;
cymbals jangle like Jack Lemmon's effeminate feet - in 1959,

descending,
          ascending.

Bill Evans, alive in this weather-sprinkled serene husk,
a live black and white tape, foggy - sweeping sonic hush
homes-in like wolves who compute their easy kills -

arriving.

You and Roger Moore

Ford Anglia, flat ballet pumps,
jungle-skinned scarf, San Tropez -
the ticklish cool-blue gusts of early June;

for my money's worth
you'll be sitting in some seaside cafe somewhere, some photo-
graph,
some Sunday, when the yachts come back for lunch,

you, Roger Moore, a few late teens -
almost meatless in Breton tops,
albino slacks;

and that Ford awaits - cherished sparkling carriage,
a saintly shine of face,
almost ascending

in a gush
of milky sun,
kitten heels soon clicked on, heavens parting;

you
and
Roger Moore

Night Scenes

Every car breaks a red light at night
every cop sits and chats with some other cop,
laughing about their halcyon days in Templemore.
A man named Tony sits alone somewhere,
there is tequila, an emptied bag of fries,
and I catch the briefest glimpse of his life walking past,
his back to me
in the beautiful mathematics of his window
like a sweaty 53 year old overweight man in a window in New York City
lying dead for the last 6, perhaps 9 hours.
And the cops are sweating and laughing outside his window,
cars breaking every red light, and his television is fat and rotund
as televisions should always be

Empirical Horizons

(1)
Schleswig-Holstein;
There's a language in that noun alone,
its dialect the prod of Heaven-stabbing soldiers' hats,
the ornate Austro-Hungarian shapes
trot in cobblestones that shine from each street corner.

(2)
At Rosenthal's candy shop
a smooth 1912 mirrored glaze
muffles the speech from officers' walrus mustaches,
freckled boys flick their fringes, strides gallant.

(3)
I've read Clifford Geertz enough to know
the signs, the teeth that chatter symphonies
on moonlit wires, the shapes of stone-faced shops -
a language no-one needs decipher -

telegraph poles that shook and stooped
with Parkinson's that
wait and glance and pause
like grandads in 1912 - feed legions of Vienna's squabbling
ducks.

(4)
I watch Chaplin's exotic shapes, that language of smile,
roguish stitched-on mustache, the Jewish boys
and Roma girls in love, tugging the maestro's lapels
in vertical swipes and soon to be widowed window panes -

and the cousins mustached for real,
a language lost in the separates of D.N.A.
send fist-shakes and dynamite-fizzled verbs
on the regrets of already-widowed tightrope telegraph wire;

(5)
one cloud asks another - how much it rained in 1912,
a damp downfall of spit-frizzled word -
in Schleswig-Holstein, Vienna,
and Yugoslav boys who walk up and down the Latin Bridge -

thinking of those next few summers

We Walk Through Dublin Late on Fridays,
Annette and Me

The sky is softness
our hair translates,
that the breeze enunciates;

when we look up at Capricorn
as mothers and fathers of stars,
we watch the bitter tug of empty glass

fall out in an troop
of untrained sunsets,
like the bar behind us

has lost its
time,
crawling towards us -

its nails are sheared on concrete sidewalks, and its stars are
bleeding, lifeless;
its lives to the count of nine
let one more life go -

when we look at stars
they pull us upwards
as children do for seasoned parents,

shopping, washing, feeding
giving light to stars
lost on Fridays

on cities

we live and love and breed in,
the fallen armies

in shut down
bars
bound-up behind us, stars as flecks on graffiti's John Hancock

Wicklow Heathers

And there's only one meadow's way to go/And you say "Geronimo"
—Van Morrison "Fair Play" 1974

Firewood gathering presses on,
auburn, almost hourglass woman, man
a figure cut from heel-deepened moss;

approaching lake an abundance crackles -
where moistened dungarees
on late-born ewes herald spring on August moors.

The glen's fading lights
freeze shadows
lingering on the bounty of prams, the day

swelling in the glow of Autumn cheek,
a sequel scripted traces
gently - palmed on this oval ad-libbed bump -

the tyre-ping of scattered pebble
and a rusty-gate's clang
upwards; up towards their sudden citadel

"A Fair Swathe of Land..."

"You venture a fair swathe of land
to reach those masts from here",
I carve a pipe-smoke misted man, entangled in fence before me,
muttering words
through his woodbine-coughed leanings;
close as they seem those masts,
close
as heart appears to be to its misgivings,
magic and gold like Yukon re-lived,
the clink and chatter of weekend glass,
and the gold rush of girls cuddled in aboriginal Clancy Brothers wool;
aye, you venture a fair swathe of land
for gold, for sullen riverbank lead,
out by Glenmalure, deep in a countryside's Sunday squelch, water,
light, being all

Pski's Porch Publishing was formed July 2012, to make books for people who like people who like books. We hope we have some small successes. **www.pskisporch.com**.

323 East Avenue
Lockport, NY 14094
www.pskisporch.com

64874161R00050

Made in the USA
Middletown, DE
31 August 2019